THE LETTERS OF PAUL AS RITUALS OF WORSHIP

The Letters of Paul
as Rituals of Worship

JOHN PAUL HEIL

CASCADE *Books* · Eugene, Oregon

Cascade Books
An Imprint of Wipf and Stock Publishers
199 W. 8th Ave., Suite 3
Eugene, OR 97401

www.wipfandstock.com

ISBN 13: 978-1-60899-870-8

Cataloging-in-Publication data:

Heil, John Paul

    The letters of Paul as rituals of worship / John Paul Heil.

    viii + 208 p. ; 23 cm. — Includes bibliographical references and indexes.

    ISBN 13: 978-1-60899-870-8

    1. Bible. N.T. Epistles of Paul—Criticism, interpretation, etc. 2. Worship—Biblical teaching. I. Title.

BS2650.52 H45 2011

Manufactured in the U.S.A.

Contents

Abbreviations · *vii*

Introduction: The Letters of Paul as Rituals of Worship · 1

1 Thessalonians · 5

2 Thessalonians · 17

1 Corinthians · 28

2 Corinthians · 50

Galatians · 64

Romans · 75

Philemon · 95

Colossians · 100

Ephesians · 121

Philippians · 137

Titus · 154

1 Timothy · 160

2 Timothy · 171

Conclusion: The Letter of Paul as Rituals of Worship · 179

Bibliography · 183

Scripture Index · 193

Author Index · 205

Abbreviations

AB	Anchor Bible
ABR	*Australian Biblical Review*
AnBib	Analecta biblica
BBR	*Bulletin for Biblical Research*
BECNT	Baker Exegetical Commentary on the New Testament
Bib	*Biblica*
BIS	Biblical Interpretation Series
BJRL	*Bulletin of the John Rylands University Library of Manchester*
BNTC	Black's New Testament Commentaries
BT	*The Bible Translator*
BZNW	Beihefte zur Zeitschrift für die neutestamentliche Wissenschaft
CBQ	*Catholic Biblical Quarterly*
EBib	*Etudes bibliques*
EDNT	*Exegetical Dictionary of the New Testament*. Edited by H. Balz, G. Schneider. ET. Grand Rapids, 1990–1993
HUT	Hermeneutische Untersuchungen zur Theologie
ICC	International Critical Commentary
JBL	*Journal of Biblical Literature*
JECS	*Journal of Early Christian Studies*
JSNT	*Journal for the Study of the New Testament*
JSNTSup	Journal for the Study of the New Testament: Supplement Series
JTS	*Journal of Theological Studies*

LNTS	Library of New Testament Studies
Neot	*Neotestamentica*
NIBCNT	New International Biblical Commentary on the New Testament
NICNT	New International Commentary on the New Testament
NIGTC	New International Greek Testament Commentary
NovT	*Novum Testamentum*
NovTSup	Supplements to Novum Testamentum
NTL	New Testament Library
NTM	New Testament Monographs
NTS	*New Testament Studies*
PRSt	*Perspectives in Religious Studies*
RB	*Revue biblique*
RevExp	*Review and Expositor*
SBLAbib	Society of Biblical Literature Academia Biblica
SBLECL	Society of Biblical Literature Early Christianity and Its Literature
SBLSCS	Society of Biblical Literature Septuagint and Cognate Studies
SNTSMS	Society for New Testament Studies Monograph Series
SP	Sacra Pagina
TNTC	Tyndale New Testament Commentaries
TynBul	*Tyndale Bulletin*
WBC	Word Biblical Commentary
WUNT	Wissenschaftliche Untersuchungen zum Neuen Testament
ZNW	*Zeitschrift für die neutestamentliche Wissenschaft und die Kunde der älteren Kirche*

Introduction:
The Letters of Paul as Rituals of Worship

We rightly consider Paul, a Jew from Tarsus who became the apostle to the Gentiles, as a great missionary, evangelist, teacher, preacher, and pastor.[1] We often neglect, however, to give him the full consideration he deserves as the preeminent and paradigmatic person of prayer and worship.[2] Our most direct access to Paul is through the letters attributed to him. Yet when we read and listen to these letters, we often overlook their original function as epistolary rituals of worship. They were originally performed publicly in a liturgical assembly. They framed the issues and problems that Paul addressed through them within a context of communal worship. They aimed to enable and facilitate the worship of the assembly, not only their liturgical worship in the particular gathering in which they listened to the letter, but the ethical or moral worship of their everyday lives outside of the liturgical assembly.

1. For a recent comprehensive and perceptive presentation of Paul the missionary, see Schnabel, *Paul the Missionary*.

2. "Worship in the NT usually means expression of praise or thanksgiving. Sometimes it implies obeisance as an attitude for supplication. In any case, it is the appropriate human response to the magnificent glory of God" (Powell, "Worship, New Testament," 1391). "Worship characteristically involves ritualized actions . . . expressions of praise and adoration and also appeals directed to a deity, the devotee(s) usually expressing subordination to and/or dependence on the intended recipient of worship while also affirming a positive relationship with the recipient" (Hurtado, "Worship, NT Christian," 910–11).

1

Epistolary Rituals of Worship

What, more specifically, does it mean to recognize Paul's letters as "epistolary rituals of worship"?[3] First, the original setting for the public performance of these letters was communal worship that was most likely connected to the celebration of the Eucharist.[4] Their audiences listened to the theological concepts, particular problems, and pressing concerns Paul addressed to them, as they were gathered together, probably in house churches, for worship.[5] Even the letters addressed to individual delegates of Paul—Titus and Timothy—were not purely personal letters but were also addressed to the worshiping community as a whole.

Secondly, ritualistic and liturgical language both frames and permeates the letters of Paul. Each of the thirteen letters of Paul begins and ends with the same ritualistic greeting that "grace be with you"—the divine grace that comes from God the Father and/or the Lord Jesus Christ. This initial greeting of "grace" sets a liturgical tone for the letter that follows, a tone that is often prolonged by Paul's pronouncements of thanksgiving and/or blessing that serve as an epistolary worship of God, along with assurances of his prayers for his audience. In other words, Paul worships within the letters themselves, thanking, praising, and praying to God for the benefit of those listening. In addition, Paul often refers to the liturgical worship of his audience, their singing of psalms, spiritual songs, hymns, etc., and requests that they reciprocate his prayers with prayers of their own for his benefit. Furthermore, Paul often employs the cultic language that describes the suitability of sacrificial victims, terms such as "holy, blameless, and without blemish," when he exhorts his audiences on how they are to extend their worship beyond their liturgical assembly and into their everyday lives, how their moral living is to be an act of worship.[6]

3. "Ritual" is used here in the sense of "the observance of set forms or rites, as in public worship," as listed in *Webster's New World Dictionary*, 1229. See also DeMaris, *Ritual World*.

4. With regard to the letters of Paul, "the presence of liturgical formulas (greeting, prayers, blessings, fragments of hymns) are unmistakable signs that they were meant to be presented to communities at assemblies connected with the celebration of the Eucharist" (Farkasfalvy, "Eucharistic Provenance," 28).

5. Balch, "Rich Pompeiian Houses," 27–46; Harland, "House Church," 903.

6. On the use of cultic language in the letters of Paul, see Vahrenhorst, *Kultische Sprache*; Finlan, *Paul's Cultic Atonement Metaphors*.

Thirdly, as substitutes for his personal presence, the letters of Paul make him present to his various audiences in and through his words of worship considered as ritual "speech acts," that is, words that actually do what they say, words that communicate by not only informing but performing.[7] For example, when his audiences hear Paul's greeting of God's grace, they begin to have a renewed awareness of that grace as an expression that epitomizes the freely given, gracious salvation God has accomplished for them in the death and resurrection of the Lord Jesus Christ. When his audiences hear Paul praying for them in his letters, his prayers have a performative effect within the rhetorical strategy, as they make him part of, indeed the epistolary presider of, their communal worship. His prayers, then, begin to take effect in the very hearing of them by his audiences. When his audiences hear Paul praising and glorifying God in his letters, they are drawn into his own worship, inspired to imitate him as the preeminent and paradigmatic person of prayer, as one who worships God the Father and our Lord Jesus Christ not only in a liturgical assembly but in and through his everyday living.

Worship and the Letters of Paul

Some of the elements and dimensions of worship have been analyzed and studied in various letters of Paul.[8] But I am not aware of any treatment focusing solely on these letters from the aspect of worship in a comprehensive way.[9] Indeed, in my opinion, the aspect of worship has been largely neglected or undervalued in New Testament studies in general.[10] Although there have been numerous investigations of the letters of Paul from the aspect of their historical context, theology, rhetoric, ethics, social and political context, etc., scholars rarely if ever devote

7. On "speech act" theory in general, see Austin, *How to Do Things with Words*.

8. See, for example, Schubert, *Pauline Thanksgiving*; Wiles, *Paul's Intercessory Prayers*; O'Brien, *Introductory Thanksgivings*; Fowl, *Hymnic Material*.

9. An overview of each of the letters of Paul, however, is included in a more general treatment of worship in the entire New Testament by Borchert, *Worship in the New Testament*.

10. For some exceptions to this neglect, see Peterson, *Engaging with God*; Hurtado, *Origins of Christian Worship*; idem, *Lord Jesus Christ*; idem, *How on Earth*; Neyrey, *Give God the Glory*; idem, "Lost in Translation," 1–23; Borchert, *Worship in the New Testament*.

serious consideration to the aspect of communal worship that provides the context, framework, and much of the content of these letters. The worship aspect so central to these letters seems to have been largely taken for granted and/or ignored, and has thus more or less faded into a shadowy background.

This book aims to contribute toward the correction of this deficiency by focusing on the aspect of worship in the letters of Paul in an effort to shed some light upon this key feature and bring the various dimensions of its significance closer to the foreground of Pauline studies. It will treat each of the thirteen New Testament letters attributed to Paul solely and exclusively from the aspect of worship, understood in its most comprehensive sense from the biblical tradition that combines in a dynamic interrelationship both liturgical and ethical worship. The intended outcome is a fresh way of reading and listening to the letters of Paul for a deeper appreciation of their original purpose. The goal is not to replace or contradict previous studies of Paul's letters but to supplement and hopefully enrich them. I now invite you to join me in what I hope will prove to be a very enlightening and stimulating survey of the letters of Paul as epistolary rituals of worship.[11]

11. The order to be followed for this survey of the letters of Paul will not be the canonical order that places Romans first and Philemon last. Rather, a chronological order that holds 1 Thessalonians to have been written first and 2 Timothy last will be followed. Although there is no consensus on the exact order in which the letters were written, there seems to be a more or less general agreement distinguishing those letters written early from those written later in the Pauline mission. All biblical translations in the following chapters are my own.

1 Thessalonians

According to the Acts of the Apostles, after Paul and Silas left Philippi, they eventually arrived in another city in the region of Macedonia, namely, Thessalonica, where they preached the gospel about Jesus as the Christ in a synagogue of the Jews (Acts 17:1–3). Some of the Jews were persuaded and joined Paul and Silas, along with a large group of God-fearing Greeks and several prominent women (17:4). But other Jews stirred up a crowd against Paul and Silas, so that they had to be sent to another Macedonian city, Beroea, where they made more converts (17:5–12). But when the Jews of Thessalonica heard that the word of God was proclaimed by Paul in Beroea, they came there as well, inciting and stirring up the crowds (17:13). As a result, Paul was sent to the seacoast, while Silas and Timothy remained behind (17:14). Those who accompanied Paul led him as far as Athens, and then returned with an order for Silas and Timothy to join Paul as soon as possible (17:15). After preaching in Athens with limited success (17:16–34), Paul went on to the Achaian city of Corinth (18:1), where he stayed for a year and six months, teaching the word of God (18:11). It is most probably during this time (49–50 CE) from Corinth that the first letter to the Thessalonians was sent, which is generally believed to be the earliest of Paul's surviving letters.[1]

The letter presents itself as being sent by Paul, Silvanus (=Silas), and Timothy to the *ekklēsia*, the "church" or "assembly," of the Thessalonians (1 Thess 1:1). But the several references to Paul alone (2:18; 3:5; 5:27) indicate that he is the primary author who dictated the letter.[2] Noteworthy is the parental imagery that portrays the authors'

---

1. Ascough, "Thessalonians, First Letter," 569; Fee, *Thessalonians*, 3–5.
2. Ascough, "Thessalonians, First Letter," 571; Fee, *Thessalonians*, 4.

close relationship with their audience: "with affection for you like a nursing mother caring for her own children" (2:7–8);[3] "we treated each one of you as a father treats his own children" (2:11); and "when we left you as orphans . . . we became all the more eager in our great desire to see you in person" (2:17).[4]

The fundamental Pauline triad of faith, love, and hope appears near the beginning (1:3) and near the end (5:8) of the letter. "Faith" (*pistis*) for Paul is the acceptance of divine grace by submitting one-self in obedience and trust to the eschatological saving activity of God initiated by the life, death, and resurrection of Jesus Christ. "Love" (*agapē*) within the triad is inspired by and flows from faith. It refers to the sincere, mutual, and presently active care and concern for one's fellow believer in response to God's love for us as manifested in the death and resurrection of Jesus Christ. Based upon faith in what God has accomplished in the Christ event, "hope" (*elpis*) for Paul is an absolutely assured, confident, and firm expectation of participating in the future and final salvation of God.

While Timothy has brought back to Paul good news of the faith and love of the Thessalonians (3:6), there is yet a need to correct some "deficiencies" in their faith (3:10). Since their faith and love but not their hope have been affirmed, this suggests that there is something not quite right with regard to their hope that is to be based upon their faith. In other words, their faith is apparently somewhat deficient with regard to the hope it should establish. The letter thus aims to encourage the Thessalonians with the proper and assured hope they should have for those who have already died before the final coming of Christ (4:13–18), as they await its unknown time of arrival by being "clothed with the breastplate of faith and love, and as a helmet the hope of salvation" (5:8). The hope the letter gives them thus caps off their faith and love that the letter affirms.[5]

---

3. Gaventa, *Our Mother Saint Paul*, 17–28.

4. Fee, *Thessalonians*, 105.

5. "In 1 Thessalonians the triad is used with different images; in the first instance with work-related images (work, labor, endurance) and in the second case with images taken from military armor (breastplate, helmet). Faith and love are mentioned together in 3:6 with reference to the Thessalonians (compare 3:10), and in 4:13 Paul seeks to address an issue that has the potential to cause them to lose hope: the death of loved ones. Elsewhere in the letter the words or their cognates are used frequently,

1 Thessalonians as a Ritual of Worship

Introductory Worship

With the opening greeting of "grace to you and peace," the authors of the letter affirm the divine grace and peace that the Thessalonians have already received as a church or assembly of believers who now live within a divine realm or sphere characterized as their being "in God the Father and the Lord Jesus Christ" (1:1).[6] This initial greeting also functions as a prayer that the Thessalonians, gathered as a "church" or "assembly" (*ekklēsia*) for worship, have a renewed and ongoing experience of this divine grace and peace both during and after they have listened to the letter within their liturgical gathering.[7]

The authors then perform an act of epistolary worship that acknowledges the divine "grace" (*charis*) the Thessalonians have been given—"we thank (*eucharistoumen*) God always concerning all of you" (1:2a). They thank God not only now in the letter but always, as they make mention of the Thessalonians in their prayers, constantly (1:2b). More specifically, they call to mind in their prayers before our God and Father the manifestation of the fundamental triad of faith, love, and hope on the part of the Thessalonians—"your work of faith and labor of love and endurance of hope in our Lord Jesus Christ" (1:3).[8]

---

suggesting that the three elements of faith, hope, and love reflect the social and ethical standards to which the Thessalonian Jesus-believers aspire" (Ascough, "Thessalonians, First Letter," 574).

6. "[I]t is likely that Paul combined 'grace' with the Jewish 'peace' to create a new form of epistolary address appropriate to his purpose and the setting in which he thought the letter would be read. The setting he had in mind was the congregation at worship, and . . . one function it would perform was liturgical" (Malherbe, *Thessalonians*, 100). "Far from being a mere formality, in Paul's hands the common letter greeting becomes a blessing that embraces the totality of the divine benefits he and his associates desire for the Christians in Thessalonica" (Green, *Thessalonians*, 86).

7. The term "church" (*ekklēsia*) refers "not to a building but to the active gathering together of believers for worship and fellowship. One might translate it here 'the gathered assembly of Thessalonians in God.' This reminds us once more that this letter was to be read out when the gathered assembly met for worship. It is addressed to the body at corporate worship and was not meant primarily for private reading like a personal letter might be" (Witherington, *Thessalonians*, 49–50).

8. "Paul's concentrated use of labials at the beginning of his first thanksgiving shows that he is writing with a view of how the letter would sound when read aloud. The letter would therefore function as a speech, and the liturgical features in these first

As the opening thanksgiving section continues, the authors further affirm the faith of the Thessalonians. They relate that other believers, those not only in Macedonia and Achaia but in every place that the faith of the Thessalonians has gone forth (1:8), are reporting how "you turned to God from idols to serve the living and true God" (1:9). That the Thessalonians have turned to God from idols means that they have abandoned their former idolatrous worship. The reference to their "service" thus implies a new worship that includes both their liturgical and ethical worship of the living and true God. Such worship is based on their faith in the living and true God who raised his Son from the dead, and it includes the hope of awaiting this Son from heaven, the Jesus who delivers us from the coming wrath (1:10).[9]

Worship in the Body of the Letter

That not only the Thessalonians but God himself is a witness to how "devoutly and justly and blamelessly" the authors became toward them as those who believe (2:10) describes an ethical worship approved by God. As part of their very close and personal relationship with the Thessalonians (2:8), the authors treated each of them "as a father treats his own children" (2:11). This fatherly instruction included exhorting and encouraging them "to walk," that is, to conduct their lives, worthily of the God who is calling them into his kingdom and glory (2:12). For

---

verses contribute to the character of the speech as a sermon. Paul's epistolary thanksgivings may indeed reflect his practice of beginning his sermons with such a prayer. The worshipful tone already established in the salutation is now continued. This report of the thanksgiving Paul constantly gives is the first of five prayers or prayer reports in the letter (1:2–3; 2:13; 3:10; 3:11–13; 5:23), which appear in important places in the structure of the letter and make the letter different from ordinary friendly letters" (Malherbe, *Thessalonians*, 122–23). "References to health wishes and even prayer and worship were also not uncommon in ancient letters. . . . It is striking, however, that Paul's tone in 1 Thessalonians is equally worshipful and respectful even though Paul writes as a religious and social superior (or at least as equal) to his converts" (Witherington, *Thessalonians*, 56).

9. "Converts 'serve' the God who is living and true, implying the lordship of the living God. Implied here is the notion that Gentile conversion entailed a change of lordships, moving from bondage to pagan gods to a new life rendered in service to the living God. In Jewish tradition also, monotheism entails being a 'servant' to the living God and 'service' entailed both worship and adherence to the commandments" (Goodwin, *Apostle of the Living God*, 115).

the Thessalonians to conduct their lives "worthily" of God amounts to offering their own ethical worship as a worthy response to the grace of God, here described as God graciously calling them into his kingdom and glory.[10]

Furthermore, that the Thessalonians have received the word of God from the authors not as a word of human beings but, as it truly is, the word of God, inspires the authors to the worship of thanking God constantly (2:13a). That "we thank God constantly" recalls and reinforces the authors' initial act of worship—"we thank God always concerning all of you, making mention of you in our prayers, constantly" (1:2). That the word of God that the Thessalonians received from the authors is at work in them as those who are believing (2:13b) empowers their ethical worship of "walking worthily" of God (2:12). By such ethical worship that is energized by the word of God, the Thessalonians may thus follow the lead of the authors and offer the worthy worship of likewise thanking God constantly.[11]

Having been encouraged that the Thessalonians are still standing firm in their faith (3:7–8), the authors are prompted to an especially joyous worship of God in response. Indeed, "for all the joy" with which they are "rejoicing" before God because of the Thessalonians, they scarcely seem capable of rendering an adequate thanksgiving to God (3:9). The rhetorical question, "for what thanksgiving can we render to God concerning you?" (3:9a), recalls and reinforces the thanksgivings to God for the audience that the authors have already reported (1:2; 2:13). Not being able to offer adequate thanks to God has, nevertheless, not prevented the authors from the worship of thanking God and rejoicing with all joy before God because of the faith of the Thessalonians.[12]

Yet the deficiencies that remain in the faith of the Thessalonians have caused the authors to turn to a different kind of worship. Night and day they are praying exceedingly to see the Thessalonians in person

---

10. "The moral life of a person was frequently described as the way one 'walked,' both in the OT and in Hellenistic literature. This language is adopted in the NT, especially in the Pauline letters, to speak of the way one conducts oneself—either before God or in sin" (Green, *Thessalonians*, 137).

11. "The view that the moral life is to be congruent with God is characteristically Jewish and Christian" (Malherbe, *Thessalonians*, 152).

12. "The rhetorical question signifies that, while it is appropriate to render thanks to God, it could not be done adequately" (ibid., 204).

in order to remedy these deficiencies in their faith (3:10). That these deficiencies are the cause of such an intense worship of petitionary prayer underlines their seriousness and prepares the audience for hearing them addressed within the letter itself as a substitute for the personal presence of Paul and his coauthors.[13]

An example of the authors' frequent praying to see the audience in order to correct their faith is then provided for their encouragement: "May God himself, our Father, and our Lord Jesus direct our way to you, and may the Lord cause you to increase and abound in love for one another and for all, just as we for you, so as to strengthen your hearts to be blameless in holiness before our God and Father at the coming of our Lord Jesus with all his holy ones" (3:11–13).[14] This increase in love (cf. 1:3; 3:6) will enable the Thessalonians to offer the proper ethical worship of being "blameless in holiness" (3:13), like a worthy sacrificial offering, before our God and Father at the final coming of the Lord Jesus.[15]

As the deficiencies in the faith of the Thessalonians (3:10) begin to be addressed, the authors request that as their audience received from

13. According to Green (*Thessalonians*, 173), "their prayers were not simple requests since the verb (participle) translated *we pray* (*deomenoi*) means 'to pray with insistence' or 'implore.'"

14. On the presence of an "amen" at the conclusion of the prayer in some manuscripts, see Metzger, *Textual Commentary*, 563. "It is hard to imagine the circumstances in which so many early and excellent witnesses would have omitted it had it been original" (Fee, *Thessalonians*, 128n4).

15. "The extended introductory thanksgiving of 1:2—3:13 is one of the most distinctive formal features of 1 Thessalonians. We propose that its presence in the letter is intended to reassure the community by establishing the soundness of the ground for his initial thanksgiving (1:2–3) in the face of the eschatological confusion and its ramifications and of Thessalonian concerns about the missionaries on account of their extended absence" (Nicholl, *From Hope to Despair*, 99n40). According to Witherington (*Thessalonians*, 104–5), "the prayer for growth in love is part and parcel with the prayer for holiness since increasing in love amounts to increasing in holiness and moves toward the goal of blamelessness. . . . The Thessalonians' coming to be 'established without blame in holiness' means that they will be conformed to the character of God himself." Fee (*Thessalonians*, 129) notes, "Paul records a prayer for them that seems to have two purposes. First, he hereby concludes the narrative of his and the Thessalonians' past and present relationships on a note similar to, and thus forming a kind of inclusio with, the prayer of thanksgiving with which the letter began (1:2–3). At the same time, second, he anticipates the matters addressed in the rest of the letter, where he deals with the 'deficiencies' mentioned at the end of the preceding sentence (v. 10)."

them how they must "walk and please God," as indeed they are "walking," so they should do so even more (4:1). This is a request that their "walking," that is, the way they conduct their lives morally, be an ethical worship that "pleases God." Their moral conduct, then, should stand in contrast to those Judean Jews who killed the Lord Jesus and the prophets and persecuted Paul and others (2:15a). By such conduct these Jews did not "please God" and were opposed to all human beings (2:15b). The Thessalonians are thus to follow the example of Paul and his coauthors, who speak the gospel with which they were entrusted not to please human beings, but as a sincere ethical worship that "pleases God," who examines their hearts (2:4). The ethical worship of the Thessalonians includes the maintenance of their holiness—"for this is the will of God," which they may do by avoiding sexual immorality (4:3). For God did not call us to impurity but to holiness (4:7; cf. 2:12), the holiness that is to embrace their entire way of living and thus render ethical worship that is pleasing to God.[16]

One of the deficiencies in the faith of the Thessalonians (3:10) involves a lack in the hope that is based on their faith. They do not seem to possess a hope that those who have already "fallen asleep," that is, died, will participate in the final coming of the Lord Jesus. But they are reassured, and may encourage one another, that those who have already died will indeed be raised to meet the Lord when he comes again (4:13–18).

But having a proper hope also includes avoiding the complacency of those who are not aware of and ready for the sudden and unexpected coming of the Day of the Lord (5:1–3). The Thessalonians are thus exhorted to live in faith, love, and hope, as these basic Christian attitudes provide believers with the protective "armor" needed to meet the destructive dangers surrounding this unexpected coming (5:4–8). As a protective "helmet," hope assures that whether believers are now "awake," that is, "alive and alert" spiritually and morally, or "asleep," that is, "dead" spiritually and morally, at the final coming of Christ they will

---

16. "'Pleasing God' does not mean anything so mundane as 'being pleasant' toward him but rather points to serving him in a way that makes his interests a person's primary ambition" (Green, *Thessalonians*, 185). "God's calling of the Thessalonians to himself was for the purpose of their living 'in holiness,' meaning that 'holiness' was to be the context that framed all of life both within and outside the community of faith" (Fee, *Thessalonians*, 152).

receive salvation and participate with him in eternal "life" (5:9–10). In the event that believers are morally "asleep," they need to be "awakened" to a life of holiness by repenting with the encouragement and edification of their fellow Christians (5:11). Such moral alertness amounts to the ethical worship that pleases God (4:1).[17]

Worship in the Letter's Closing

As the letter begins to come to a close, the Thessalonians are exhorted to "rejoice always" (5:16). They are thus invited to join in the joyous worship of the authors inspired by the faith of the Thessalonians—"for all the joy with which we are rejoicing because of you before our God" (3:9). The Thessalonians are exhorted to "constantly pray" (5:17) and "in everything to give thanks, for this is the will of God for you in Christ Jesus" (5:18).[18] They are thus called to imitate the manner of worship performed by the authors, who are thanking God constantly (2:13), thanking God always for all of the Thessalonians, remembering them in their prayers, constantly (1:2). When the Thessalonians are gathered for worship, they are not to quench the Spirit (5:19), which may be speaking to them in prophecies they are not to despise from fellow participants (5:20). They should examine all such prophetic utterances and retain what is beneficial to the community (5:21). And as part of their ethical worship, they are to refrain from every form of evil (5:22).

At the beginning of the letter the authors prayed that the "peace" of God be granted to the Thessalonians (1:1). Now the authors pray to the "God of peace" to bring the ethical worship of the Thessalonians to its completion at the final coming of the Lord: "May the God of peace himself make you completely holy, and may your entire spirit and soul and body be kept blameless at the coming of our Lord Jesus Christ. Faithful is the one calling you, who indeed will accomplish it" (5:23–24). The God who did not "call" the Thessalonians to moral impurity

---

17. Heil, "1 Thess 5.9–10," 464–71.

18. "Practicing this kind of prayer in the midst of extreme social pressure is only possible on the basis of, and would exemplify, an utter dependence on God and the hope of God's coming public vindication of the faithful (as Paul describes in 4:13–5:11). It would both flow from, and continue to engender, a transformation of this audience's imagination" (Johnson, "Sanctification," 288).

but to "holiness" (4:7), the "holiness" that is the will of God as their ethical worship (4:3), is the God who is "calling" them into his own kingdom and glory, as those conducting themselves in the ethical worship that is worthy of God (2:12). This is the faithful God "calling" the Thessalonians (5:24), the God of peace who will make them completely "holy" in their ethical worship, with their entire persons kept "blameless" (5:23), like a sacrificial offering worthy of and pleasing to God. This prayer thus resonates with and reinforces the previous prayer that the Thessalonians be "blameless in holiness" before our God and Father at the coming of our Lord Jesus Christ with all his holy ones (3:13).[19]

The Thessalonians, who were exhorted to constantly pray (5:17), are now exhorted to pray also for the authors (5:25). They are thus to reciprocate the prayers offered for their benefit by the authors. Paul and his coauthors are making mention of all of the Thessalonians in their prayers, constantly (1:2), as exemplified in the letter itself (3:10–13; 5:23–24). The Thessalonians are to greet all the brothers, as they are gathered together to listen to the reading of the letter (5:27), with the liturgical ritual of the "holy kiss" (5:26).[20] The verbless final greeting, "the grace of the Lord Jesus Christ with you" (5:28), reaffirms that the Thessalonians, as believers, have already been recipients of this divine grace. It also functions as a prayer that they will continue to experience this grace as a result of having listened to the letter. This climactic prayer

19. "Paul's wish-prayer in 5:23–24 must be understood in light of his former wish-prayer in 3:11–13 as well as in light of his concrete exhortations in 4:1–5:22. As we have seen, adherence to these concrete exhortations would result in practices that both presuppose and continue the transformation of his audience's imagination. . . . Because this God is faithful (v. 24), the result will be a people of God, kept blameless *both now and at the eschaton* because their communal life is constituted by self-giving actions" (Johnson, "Sanctification," 289–90). "With this twofold benedictory prayer Paul concludes his letter by emphasizing his two major concerns in writing: that the Thessalonian believers continue on a course of holy living; and that they do so until the Parousia itself" (Fee, *Thessalonians*, 225–26).

20. "The kiss is not an ordinary one but is to be holy, Paul again picking up on a major theme of the letter. Such a greeting may have been given at different points in the church's worship" (Malherbe, *Thessalonians*, 341). "This kiss is described as *holy*, not necessarily to distinguish it from the erotic kiss but rather to identify it with the common life of those who were 'holy ones' or 'saints.' As such, the adjective *holy* reinforces the bond between them that the kiss itself symbolizes and separates this symbol of their unity from the kisses they would exchange with others in their world" (Green, *Thessalonians*, 271). See also Penn, "Performing Family," 151–74; idem, *Kissing Christians*.

for the divine "grace" of the Lord Jesus Christ forms a literary inclusion with the opening greeting and prayer that "grace" and peace (cf. 5:23) be given to the assembly of the Thessalonians in God the Father and the Lord Jesus Christ (1:1). These opening and closing prayers for divine grace thus frame the entire letter within a context of worship.[21]

Conclusion: Worship in 1 Thessalonians

After the initial greeting of "grace to you and peace" (1:1), Paul and his coauthors perform an act of epistolary worship that acknowledges the divine "grace" the Thessalonians have been given—"we thank God always concerning all of you" (1:2a). They thank God not only now in the letter but always, as they make mention of the Thessalonians in their prayers, constantly (1:2b). That the Thessalonians have turned to God from idols means that they have abandoned their former idolatrous worship for a new "service" that includes both their liturgical and ethical worship of the living and true God (1:9).

For the Thessalonians to conduct their lives "worthily" of God amounts to them offering their own ethical worship as a worthy response to the grace of God, the God who is graciously calling them into his kingdom and glory (2:12). That the word of God which the Thessalonians received from the authors is at work in them as those who are believing (2:13b) empowers their ethical worship of "walking worthily" of God (2:12). By such ethical worship that is energized by the word of God, the Thessalonians may thus follow the lead of the authors and offer the worthy worship of likewise thanking God constantly (2:13a).

The authors' rhetorical question, "for what thanksgiving can we render to God concerning you?" (3:9a), recalls and reinforces the

---

21. "'Peace' and 'grace' from 1:1 are repeated in 5:23, 28, which enclose the final greeting" (Malherbe, *Thessalonians*, 342). "Since this document was read in worship, we may assume that the end of the letter is liturgically shaped to suit the end of the worship service" (Witherington, *Thessalonians*, 177). "It was 'grace,' God's own favor that is theirs through 'the Lord, Jesus Christ,' with which he greeted them at the beginning; and now that same 'grace' is what he wishes for them in conclusion. It is the one word in Paul's vocabulary that embraces all that God has done, and that he desires that God will do, for his Thessalonian friends through Christ Jesus" (Fee, *Thessalonians*, 233).

thanksgivings to God for the audience that the authors have already reported (1:2; 2:13). Not being able to offer adequate thanks to God has, nevertheless, not prevented the authors from the worship of thanking God and "rejoicing with all joy before God" because of the faith of the Thessalonians (3:9b). On the other hand, that the deficiencies in their faith are the cause of such an intense worship of petitionary prayer (3:10) underlines their seriousness and prepares the Thessalonians for hearing them addressed within the letter itself as a substitute for the personal presence of Paul and his coauthors. An example of the authors' frequent praying to see the Thessalonians in order to correct their faith is then provided for their encouragement: "May God himself, our Father, and our Lord Jesus direct our way to you, and may the Lord cause you to increase and abound in love for one another and for all, just as we for you, so as to strengthen your hearts to be blameless in holiness before our God and Father at the coming of our Lord Jesus with all his holy ones" (3:11–13).

As the deficiencies in the faith of the Thessalonians (3:10) begin to be addressed, the authors request that their "walking," that is, the way they conduct their lives morally, be an ethical worship that "pleases God" (4:1). The ethical worship of the Thessalonians includes the maintenance of their holiness—"for this is the will of God," which they may do by avoiding sexual immorality (4:3). For God called them to holiness (4:7; cf. 2:12), the holiness that is to embrace their entire way of living and thus render ethical worship that is pleasing to God.

One of the deficiencies in the faith of the Thessalonians (3:10) involves a lack of hope that those who have already died will participate in the final coming of the Lord Jesus. But they are reassured, and may encourage one another, that those who have already died will indeed be raised to meet the Lord when he comes again (4:13–18). But having a proper hope also includes avoiding the complacency of those who are not aware of and ready for the sudden and unexpected coming of the Day of the Lord (5:1–3). Their hope assures that whether the Thessalonians are now "awake," that is, "alive and alert" spiritually and morally, or "asleep," that is, "dead" spiritually and morally, at the final coming of Christ they will receive salvation and participate with him in eternal life (5:9–10). In the event that some of them are morally "asleep," then they need to be "awakened" to a life of holiness by repenting with the encouragement and edification of their fellow Thessalonian believers (5:11). Such moral alertness amounts to the ethical worship that pleases God (4:1).

At the closing of the letter the Thessalonians are exhorted to "rejoice always" (5:16), to "constantly pray" (5:17), and "in everything to give thanks, for this is the will of God for you in Christ Jesus" (5:18). Then the authors pray to the "God of peace," the "peace" they prayed for the Thessalonians at the beginning of the letter (1:1), to bring the ethical worship of the Thessalonians to its completion at the final coming of the Lord: "May the God of peace himself make you completely holy, and may your entire spirit and soul and body be kept blameless at the coming of our Lord Jesus Christ. Faithful is the one calling you, who indeed will accomplish it" (5:23–24). God is the faithful one calling the Thessalonians, the God of peace who will make them completely "holy" in their ethical worship, with their entire persons kept "blameless" (5:23), like a sacrificial offering worthy of and pleasing to God (cf. 3:13).

The Thessalonians are to reciprocate the prayers (5:25) offered for their benefit by the authors (5:17). They are to greet all the brothers, as they are gathered together to listen to the reading of the letter (5:27), with the liturgical ritual of the "holy kiss" (5:26). The verbless final greeting, "the grace of the Lord Jesus Christ with you" (5:28), reaffirms that the Thessalonians, as believers, have already been recipients of this divine grace. It also functions as a prayer that they will continue to experience this grace as a result of having listened to the letter. The opening and closing prayers for divine grace (1:1; 5:28) thus frame the entire letter within a context of worship.

2 Thessalonians

Although this letter, like 1 Thessalonians, presents itself as sent from Paul, Silvanus, and Timothy (2 Thess 1:1), some have denied that it is an authentic Pauline letter. One of the main reasons for this is the language about the second coming or Parousia of Christ (2:1–12), which is deemed to be uncharacteristic of Paul. They hold that the letter is pseudonymous, and that it was written at a time much later than and in a situation different from 1 Thessalonians. Such theories usually do not provide an entirely convincing historical reconstruction or scenario for the letter, either with regard to the letter's pseudonymous authorship or audience. The various theories of pseudonymity seem to be rather more problematic than theories of authenticity. And what is quite ironic for theories of pseudonymity is how much the letter itself insists that it is authentically from Paul (3:17; cf. 2:2, 15; 3:14).[1]

The view taken here is that 2 Thessalonians is indeed an authentic Pauline letter. It was in all likelihood written from Corinth shortly after 1 Thessalonians to address continuing and newly developing problems in the community. The letter addresses three main areas of concern. First, it encourages the Thessalonians to continue to persevere in the afflictions they are suffering at the hand of others (1:4–12). Second, it corrects erroneous views regarding the arrival of the eschatological coming of Christ (2:1–17). And thirdly, it exhorts and instructs regarding the continuing problem of those who refuse to earn their own living by working (3:6–15).[2]

---

1. Although some turn this emphatic insistence of authenticity on its head, and claim that it actually indicates that the letter is not authentic.

2. Malherbe, *Thessalonians*, 349–75; Ascough, "Thessalonians, Second Letter," 574–79; Fee, *Thessalonians*, 237–42.

2 Thessalonians as a Ritual of Worship

Introductory Worship

The letter is sent from Paul, Silvanus, and Timothy to the church or assembly of the Thessalonians gathered together for worship, who are characterized as being within a divine realm or sphere of existence—"in God our Father and the Lord Jesus Christ" (1:1). The authors, the primary of whom is Paul, address this audience with a greeting appropriate to their realm of existence—"grace to you and peace from God the Father and the Lord Jesus Christ" (1:2). The greeting affirms the grace and peace the Thessalonians, as believers, have already received and prepares them for a renewed experience of this divine grace and peace as they listen to the letter. It also initiates the epistolary worship, functioning as a prayer of petition that the audience continue to experience this divine grace and peace after and as a result of listening to the letter.[3]

The initial epistolary worship continues with a prayer of thanksgiving for the faith and love of the Thessalonians: "We ought to thank God always for you, brothers, as is fitting, because your faith is growing abundantly and the love of each one of you all for one another is abounding" (1:3). The expressions, "we ought to thank" and "as is fitting," have a liturgical background that enhances the appropriateness of the thanksgiving as an act worship.[4] Although thanks is given for the faith and love of the Thessalonians, the third member of the fundamental Pauline triad of faith, love, and hope is omitted. This hints at a lack of hope among the audience, but a hope that can be restored and renewed, based on their praiseworthy faith and love.[5]

3. "Paul sees himself as an emissary of both the Father and the Lord and brings greetings and peace from them both. Both are viewed as divine, and Paul sees himself as one who announces, indeed even conveys, their unmerited blessings and peace" (Witherington, *Thessalonians*, 185). "Just as the church is affirmed to exist '*in* God *our* Father and the Lord Jesus Christ,' so Paul now adds what will be found in all of his subsequent preserved letters, namely the *source* of this 'grace and peace,' 'God *the* Father and the Lord Jesus Christ'" (Fee, *Thessalonians*, 245).

4. Aus, "2 Thess 1:3," 432–38; Malherbe, *Thessalonians*, 382–83; Fee, *Thessalonians*, 247–48. "The 'ought' points to the divine, while 'as is fitting' points to the human side of the obligation. The Thessalonians' conduct had, at least in part, merited giving God thanks and thus it was fitting to give such thanks. Paul thus begins on a note of religious duty, both his own and that of his audience" (Witherington, *Thessalonians*, 188).

5. "The absence of hope from the thanksgiving is precisely what we would expect if

As this thanksgiving section of the letter continues, the Thessalonians are assured that at the revelation of the Lord Jesus from heaven God will punish those who are persecuting and afflicting them (1:4–7). These enemies will be punished when the Lord Jesus comes to be glorified in his holy ones and to be marveled at among all who believe, included among whom are the Thessalonians (1:8–10). To this end, Paul and his coauthors inform their audience of how often they pray for them, providing an instance of such praying that continues the epistolary worship: "We pray always for you, that our God may make you worthy of the calling and fulfill every desire for goodness and every work of faith in power, so that the name of our Lord Jesus may be glorified in you, and you in him, according to the grace of our God and the Lord Jesus Christ" (1:11–12).

Not only do the authors perform the worship of thanking God "always for you" because the faith of the Thessalonians is growing abundantly (1:3), but they perform the worship of praying "always for you" that God may bring to fulfillment every work of their faith (1:11). The purpose of this prayer of petition is the ethical worship of the Thessalonians—that they may be worthy of God's calling (1:11) and that their "work of faith," their conduct as believers, may "glorify" the name of our Lord Jesus. And they in turn will be blessed with glory from him (1:12a). In other words, the moral behavior of the Thessalonians as believers will render an ethical worship of "glorifying" the Lord Jesus that will include their being "glorified" by him.[6] Finally, the introductory prayer for the "grace" (*charis*) that comes from God the Father and the

---

our analysis of 2:1–3:5 is correct: the claim that the Day of the Lord had come eliminated the hope of those who embraced it. Nevertheless, the thanksgiving stresses that the other two elements of the triad, faith and love, were present among 'the Thessalonians' in abundant measure and they constituted reliable grounds for thanksgiving before God and indeed the foundation for the rebuilding of hope" (Nicholl, *From Hope to Despair*, 147–48).

6. "It is through their conduct now, as they are empowered by God, that the name of the Lord Jesus will be glorified. The *en hymin* ('in you') describes the ground of the glorifying, that is, 'by virtue of you.' . . . There is a reciprocity between Christians and Christ; they too will be glorified in him" (Malherbe, *Thessalonians*, 411). "In the midst of the Thessalonian believers' pain and suffering, Paul's prayer for them focuses ultimately on God and his glory. Yet God's glory will be manifest as he fulfills in his people the desire of this prayer. And one should never lose sight of the fact that God's glory is intimately tied to Christ's being glorified in and among his people" (Fee, *Thessalonians*, 268).

Lord Jesus Christ (1:2) is complemented by the prayer that the name of our Lord Jesus be glorified among the Thessalonians, according to the "grace" (*charin*) that comes from our God and the Lord Jesus Christ (1:12b).[7]

Worship in the Body of the Letter

With regard to the final coming of our Lord Jesus Christ and our assembling with him (2:1), the authors urge the Thessalonians not to be shaken out of their mind or frightened, either through a spirit, or a verbal message, or a letter allegedly from the authors to the effect that the Day of the Lord is already present (2:2). The Day of the Lord has not yet arrived, since "the man of lawlessness, the son of destruction," has not yet been revealed (2:3). This refers to the expectation of an apocalyptic, eschatological figure who opposes and exalts himself above every so-called god and object of worship, so as to seat himself in the temple of God, displaying himself as God (2:4). Since this expected false god as an object of false worship has not yet appeared, and even when he does, he will be destroyed by the Lord Jesus (2:8), the Thessalonians are to remain unalarmed, continuing in their performance of authentic worship, both liturgical and ethical, of the true God.

The authors continue to model such authentic worship as they offer another prayer of thanksgiving for the Thessalonians: "But we ought to thank God always for you, brothers beloved by the Lord, because God chose you as firstfruits for salvation in holiness of the Spirit and in faith in the truth. To this end, he called you through our gospel for the possession of the glory of our Lord Jesus Christ" (2:13–14). In their introductory worship the authors prayed "we ought to thank God always for you" (1:3). Now they begin this prayer of thanksgiving in the same way, but with an explicitly emphasized "we." Having informed the audience that unbelievers will be condemned (2:12), with an emphatic "we"—"but as for us, we ought to thank God always"—the authors

7. "One of the more effective ways of changing behavior is to let people overhear one's prayers for them. Like the parent who prays, 'dear Lord, if only my child would live up to his potential' while the child can overhear it, Paul here offers a public wish prayer to be read out before the congregation. Its rhetorical function is not just to convey information about Paul's prayers but also to instigate transformation" (Witherington, *Thessalonians*, 199–200).

thank God for the faith of the Thessalonians (2:13). Now the Thessalonians are addressed not just as "brothers" (1:3), but as "brothers beloved by the Lord" (2:13), in contrast to the "lawless one" whom the Lord will kill at his final coming (2:8). Whereas the authors first thanked God for the abundantly growing "faith" of the Thessalonians (1:3), they now thank God for choosing them for "salvation" in their "faith in the truth" (2:13), in contrast to those who do not "believe the truth" (2:12) and have not received the love of the "truth" in order to be "saved" (2:10).[8]

That the authors thank God for choosing the Thessalonians "as firstfruits for salvation in holiness of the Spirit and in faith in the truth" (2:13) refers to the Thessalonians' ethical worship. As "firstfruits" of the harvest of believers, the Thessalonian believers have been cultically consecrated to God to ensure a successful completion of the entire harvest. In other words, the Thessalonian believers are the "firstfruits" that will lead to others becoming believers.[9] That the Thessalonians have been consecrated as "firstfruits" to God in "holiness" refers to their being made holy by the divine Spirit, their being separated from the profane and consecrated to offer ethical worship to the sacred God by the conduct of their "faith in the truth."[10] And that God called the Thessalonians for the possession of the "glory" of our Lord Jesus Christ (2:14) recalls and reinforces the previous prayer for the ethical worship of the Thessalonians, the prayer that their "work of faith," their conduct as believers, may "glorify" the name of our Lord Jesus, and that they in turn will be given glory from him (1:12).

After exhorting the Thessalonians to stand firm and hold on to the traditions they were taught (2:15), the authors continue the epistolary worship with another prayer for the Thessalonians: "May our Lord

---

8. According to Fee (*Thessalonians*, 298), the Thessalonians would have understood 2:13-14 as "a thanksgiving to God for them, standing in stark contrast to the immediately preceding gruesome litany of judgment and condemnation on those who are persecuting them."

9. According to Green (*Thessalonians*, 326), "the Thessalonians are the 'first fruits,' an allusion to the first part of the harvest or even the first offspring of animals that are dedicated exclusively as sacred to God (Exod. 23.19; Num. 15.17-21; Deut. 12.6, 17). . . . the first of many who will be converted to God."

10. The conversion of the Thessalonians may be described in terms of their "sanctification" or "holiness," "both in its sense of their being now set apart for God's purposes and in its more ethical sense of their walking in God's ways, so as to reflect his character," according to Fee (*God's Empowering Presence*, 79).

Jesus Christ himself and God our Father, who loved us and gave us eternal encouragement and good hope in grace, encourage your hearts and strengthen them in every good work and word" (2:16–17). The prayer to God our Father, who "loved" us, that is, all of us believers, complements the divine love expressed in the previous thanksgiving to God for the Thessalonians as brothers "beloved" by the Lord (2:13). That our Lord Jesus Christ and God our Father gave us eternal encouragement and "good hope" within the realm of our being in divine grace (2:16; cf. 1:2, 12) reinforces the restoration of the "hope" of the Thessalonians, the "hope" that was not included with the other two elements of the Pauline triad—faith and love—in the initial thanksgiving (1:3).[11] The Thessalonians now share the "good hope" of all believers in the final coming of the Lord as an event that has not yet arrived (2:1–12). The prayer is thus for the hearts of the Thessalonians, as they await this final coming of the Lord in "good" hope, to be divinely encouraged and strengthened for both their ethical and liturgical worship—in every "good" work and word (2:17; cf. 1:11–12).[12]

Worship in the Letter's Closing

As the letter begins to come to a close, Paul and his coauthors request that their thanking and praying to God "for you" always (1:3, 11; 2:13) be reciprocated. They exhort the Thessalonians, "Finally, keep on praying, brothers, for us" (3:1a). Having just prayed that the hearts

11. As Nicholl (*From Hope to Despair*, 138n114) points out, the Thessalonians "need to know that they have an objectively sound basis for hope."

12. "'[H]eart' denotes the entire person, and 'work' and 'word' encompass all human activity. . . . The repetition of 'good' and its place at the end of the sentence lend emphasis to it" (Malherbe, *Thessalonians*, 442–43). "The prayer not only presents a petition to God but also serves as an implicit exhortation to the Thessalonians to live lives that are in harmony with the desire expressed in the prayer" (Green, *Thessalonians*, 333). Paul "prays for them at the end that, with the preceding explanations and argument in hand, they will indeed be encouraged so as not to be 'shaken' by the false teaching circulating among them. In praying for God and Christ to 'encourage your hearts,' Paul is concerned that both divine persons will bolster them in this time of crisis, and especially for what lies ahead of them; in further praying for God and Christ to 'strengthen you in every good deed and word,' Paul is bringing them back to everyday life. . . . Thus the prayer functions both as a form of encouragement under present duress and as (a subtle form of) exhortation regarding their perseverance under that duress" (Fee, *Thessalonians*, 309).

of the Thessalonians be encouraged and strengthened in every good work and "word" (2:17), the authors request the Thessalonians to pray for them that in their apostolic ministry the "word" of the Lord may speed on and be glorified among future believers as also among the Thessalonians (3:1b).[13] That the word of the Lord may be "glorified" is a prayer that the reception of the gospel, the good news of what God has accomplished in the life, death, and resurrection of the Lord Jesus Christ, may be an occasion for offering the worship of "glorifying" God. This prayer request thus reinforces not only the promise that when the Lord Jesus comes again he will be "glorified" in his holy ones, including the Thessalonians (1:10), but also the prayer that the name of our Lord Jesus Christ may be "glorified" in the Thessalonians as well as the Thessalonians in him (1:12).

The request includes that the Thessalonians pray that Paul and his apostolic associates may be rescued from the perverse and "evil" persons, for not all have "faith" (3:2). But "faithful" is the Lord, who, as the authors promise, will "strengthen" and guard the Thessalonians from the "evil one" (3:3). After expressing their confidence in the Lord that the Thessalonians are doing and will continue to do what the authors command them (3:4), they pray that the Lord may direct the "hearts" of the Thessalonians to the love of God and the endurance of Christ (3:5). This resonates with and reinforces the previous prayer that their "hearts" be encouraged and "strengthened" in every good work and word (2:17). The authors pray that, in contrast to those who are perishing because they have not accepted the "love" of the truth so that they may be saved (2:10), the Lord may direct the Thessalonians to the "love" of God. Having boasted in the churches of God about the "endurance" and faith of the Thessalonians in all of the persecutions and afflictions they are enduring (1:4), the authors now pray that the hearts of the Thessalonians be directed to the "endurance" of the Christ—the "endurance" modeled by the Christ and needed by the Thessalonians

---

13. "What 'remains to be said' first is a request for prayer *from* them, a request that follows nicely his own prayer *for* them (2:16–17). And here is an instance in the letter where the plural 'for us,' which has otherwise probably been primarily a polite literary plural, is almost certainly intended to refer to all three of them—Paul, Silas, and Timothy. But, typical of Paul, at issue in the Thessalonians' praying 'for us' is not for safety or health, but for the cause of the gospel itself" (Fee, *Thessalonians*, 313).

to endure their sufferings as they await in hope the final coming of the Christ (2:1, 14).[14]

At the beginning of the letter the audience heard the prayer-greeting of grace and "peace" from God the Father and the Lord Jesus Christ (1:2). Now, as part of the literary inclusion that places the entire letter in a context of worship, the letter concludes with a prayer that the Lord of "peace" himself may give the Thessalonians "peace" at all times and in every way (3:16a).[15] This double, emphatic reference to "peace" appears to be particularly pertinent and appropriate in view of the threats to the "peace"—the overall well-being and harmony of the Thessalonian community—that have been presented in the letter. Any of the three main problems addressed—the afflictions suffered at the hand of others (1:4–12), the erroneous views regarding the arrival of the final coming of Christ (2:1–17), and the continuing problem of those who refuse to earn their own living by working (3:6–15)—can diminish the "peace" within the Thessalonian community. This prayer is then quickly bolstered with the prayer-greeting that the Lord, the Lord of peace and giver of peace, who has been and still is with the Thessalonians, will continue to be with all of them (3:16b). This reinforces the letter's purpose of restoring the hope of the Thessalonians in the final coming of the Lord Jesus Christ that is yet to take place.[16]

14. "The apostle's request is that the *Lord* direct the Thessalonians' moral life in such a way that they exhibit *love* and *perseverance* (1 Thess. 1.3; 2 Thess. 1.3–4) that imitate these virtues of God the Father, who loved them, and Jesus Christ, who was steadfast in his sufferings for them. 'Act as God acts!' is the principal exhortation in Jewish and Christian ethics" (Green, *Thessalonians*, 340).

15. "The background of Paul's phrase is liturgical, but he adapts it to his own epistolary purpose. Paul visualizes the context, the congregation assembled for worship, in which the letter will be read and crafts the conclusion rhetorically to fit that context" (Malherbe, *Thessalonians*, 462). In 2 Thessalonians the word for "peace" (*eirēnē*) occurs only in 1:2 and 3:16.

16. "Paul is anticipating strained relations and prays that peace may prevail. That the addition to the peace wish has a general reference is due to its liturgical character, which in no way lessens its relevance to what precedes" (Malherbe, *Thessalonians*, 462). "The grand nature of the prayer stands in contrast with the agonizing situation that assailed this church. In the face of a social reality that appeared out of control, the founder of the church raises his eyes to the only one who is able to intervene and give the believers *peace*. The ancients recognized that it was the role of the gods to establish *peace*, but the apostle affirms that only Jesus Christ is truly the *Lord of peace*" (Green, *Thessalonians*, 358). "In light of the preceding content (God's coming judgment on their enemies; the timing of the day of the Lord; and unrest caused by the disruptive-idle), this prayer is precisely what is needed" (Fee, *Thessalonians*, 340).

The beginning of the letter listed its senders as "Paul and Silvanus and Timothy" (1:1). But that Paul has been its primary author is confirmed at the conclusion of the letter with the statement that "this greeting is in my own hand, Paul's; this is the sign in every letter; this is how I write" (3:17). This concerted stress on the letter's authenticity is necessary in view of the disturbance to the peace of the Thessalonians due to a forged letter allegedly from Paul to the effect that the day of the Lord is already present (2:2).

Forming a literary inclusion with the opening prayer-greeting of "grace to you and peace from God the Father and the Lord Jesus Christ" (1:2), the letter closes with the final prayer-greeting that the "grace" of our Lord Jesus Christ that has been and still is with the Thessalonians may continue to be with all of them (3:18). This final prayer-greeting resonates with and reinforces the previous prayer directed to our Lord Jesus Christ himself and God our Father, who loved us and gave us eternal encouragement and good hope in "grace" (2:16), as well as the previous prayer that the name of our Lord Jesus be glorified among the Thessalonians, according to the "grace" that comes from our God and the Lord Jesus Christ (1:12). The prayer for the "grace" of our Lord Jesus Christ includes preeminently the "grace" or "gift" of peace, the "peace" that the Lord of "peace" himself gives (3:16). The final prayer that the grace of our Lord Jesus Christ be "with you all" (3:18) thus emphatically bolsters the preceding prayer that the Lord, the Lord of peace who gives peace, be "with you all" (3:16), that is, with "all" of the Thessalonians as a unified community who fraternally admonish one another (3:15).[17]

---

17. "Unlike the benediction in 1 Thessalonians, this one is pronounced over *you all*, perhaps taking up again the theme of 3.15 concerning the way the church should respond to the disorderly. They are still brothers, and for that reason the blessing is pronounced over all members of the church. . . . *Grace* was the summary of everything they needed (1.2). In the midst of their sufferings and in their struggle against false teaching, they could not get by without God's *grace*" (Green, *Thessalonians*, 359–60). "It was 'grace,' God's own favor that is theirs through 'the Lord Jesus Christ,' with which he greeted them at the beginning; and now that same 'grace' is what he wishes for them in conclusion. It is the one word in Paul's vocabulary that embraces all that God has done, and that he desires that God will do, for his Thessalonian friends through Christ Jesus" (Fee, *Thessalonians*, 342).

Conclusion: Worship in 2 Thessalonians

The initial greeting of "grace to you and peace from God the Father and the Lord Jesus Christ" (1:2) functions as a prayer of petition that the audience continue to experience divine grace and peace after and as a result of listening to the letter in their liturgical assembly. Although the authors give thanks to God for the faith and love of the Thessalonians, a mention of their hope is notably omitted, hinting at a lack of hope among the audience, but a hope that can be restored and renewed, based on their praiseworthy faith and love.

Not only do the authors perform the worship of thanking God "always for you" because the faith of the Thessalonians is growing abundantly (1:3), but they perform the worship of praying "always for you" that God may bring to fulfillment every work of their faith (1:11). The purpose of this prayer of petition is the ethical worship of the Thessalonians. Their moral behavior as believers will render an ethical worship of "glorifying" the Lord Jesus that will include their being "glorified" by him (1:12a). The introductory prayer for the "grace" that comes from God the Father and the Lord Jesus Christ (1:2) is complemented by the prayer that the name of our Lord Jesus be glorified among the Thessalonians, according to the "grace" that comes from our God and the Lord Jesus Christ (1:12b).

Since "the man of lawlessness, the son of destruction"—the expected false god as an object of false worship—has not yet appeared (2:3–4), and even when he does, he will be destroyed by the Lord Jesus (2:8), the Thessalonians are to remain unalarmed, continuing in their performance of authentic worship, both liturgical and ethical, of the true God. The authors thank God for choosing the Thessalonians for "salvation" in their "faith in the truth" (2:13), in contrast to those who do not "believe the truth" (2:12), and have not received the love of the "truth" in order to be "saved" (2:10). That the Thessalonians have been consecrated as "firstfruits" to God in "holiness" refers to their being made holy by the divine Spirit to offer ethical worship to the sacred God by the conduct of their "faith in the truth" (2:13).

The prayer addressed to our Lord Jesus Christ and God our Father who gave us eternal encouragement and "good hope" within the realm of our being in divine grace (2:16) reinforces the restoration of the "hope" of the Thessalonians. It prays that the hearts of the Thessalonians, as they await this final coming of the Lord in "good" hope, be divinely encouraged and strengthened for both their ethical and liturgical worship—in every "good" work and word (2:17).

The authors request the Thessalonians to pray for them that in their apostolic ministry the word of the Lord may speed on and be glorified among future believers as also among the Thessalonians (3:1). That the word of the Lord may be "glorified" serves as a prayer that the reception of the gospel may be an occasion for offering the worship of "glorifying" God. The authors pray that the hearts of the Thessalonians be directed to the "endurance" of the Christ (3:5)—the "endurance" modeled by the Christ and needed by the Thessalonians to endure their sufferings as they await in hope the final coming of the Christ (2:1, 14).

As part of the literary inclusion that places the entire letter in a context of worship, the letter that commenced with the prayer-greeting of grace to you and "peace" from God the Father and the Lord Jesus Christ (1:2), concludes with a prayer that the Lord of "peace" himself may give the Thessalonians "peace" at all times and in every way (3:16a). The double, emphatic reference to "peace" in this prayer appears to be particularly pertinent and appropriate in view of the threats to the "peace" that have been presented in the letter (1:4–12; 2:1–17; 3:6–15). This prayer is bolstered with the prayer-greeting that the Lord, the Lord of peace and giver of peace, who has been and still is with the Thessalonians, will continue to be with all of them (3:16b).

Completing the literary inclusion with the opening prayer-greeting of "grace" to you and peace from God the Father and the Lord Jesus Christ (1:2), the letter closes with the final prayer-greeting that the "grace" of our Lord Jesus Christ that has been and still is with the Thessalonians may continue to be with all of them (3:18). This prayer for the "grace" of our Lord Jesus Christ includes preeminently the "grace" or "gift" of peace, the "peace" that only the Lord of "peace" himself can give (3:16). The final prayer that the grace of our Lord Jesus Christ be "with you all" (3:18) emphatically bolsters the preceding prayer-greeting that the Lord be "with you all" (3:16), that is, with "all" of the Thessalonians as a unified community who fraternally admonish one another (3:15).

1 Corinthians

Paul is in Ephesus, where he plans on staying until the Jewish feast of Pentecost, when he sends what has come to be designated as his first letter to the Corinthians (1 Cor 16:8). During his second missionary journey he had established a community in Corinth (Acts 18:1–18), where he stayed for a year and a half, teaching among them the word of God (18:11). While in Ephesus Paul was informed by those associated with a certain woman named Chloe that there were rivalries among the believers at Corinth (1 Cor 1:10–11). These rivalries, as well as a number of other issues that Paul addresses, most of which touch on matters involving worship, provide the occasion for the letter.[1]

1 Corinthians as a Ritual of Worship

Worship in 1 Corinthians 1–4

Having established his authority as one called to be an apostle of Christ Jesus through the will of God, Paul, together with the fellow believer named Sosthenes (1:1; cf. Acts 18:17), addresses the letter to the *ekklēsia* of God, the church of God, that is in Corinth assembled for worship (1:2a).[2] That this Corinthian church of God is composed of those who have been sanctified or made holy by God in Christ Jesus, those called

---

1. For a discussion of what we know about Paul's relationship with the Corinthians from his letters as compared with the Acts of the Apostles, see Phillips, *Paul, His Letters, and Acts*, 157–89.

2. "Assembly for worship is the center and at the same time the criterion for life in the church" (Roloff, "*ekklēsia*," 413). "Whatever the origin, the word [*ekklēsia*] stresses the call *to assemble together as a congregation* in God's presence" (Thiselton, *Corinthians*, 75, emphasis original).

to be holy ones (1:2b), that is, those who have been specially separated from the rest of their society and consecrated to God, qualifies them to offer worthy worship to God.[3] As those "called" to be holy ones, together with Paul "called" to be an apostle, they appropriately respond to the call of God by "calling upon" the name of our Lord Jesus Christ in worship. That they are associated with all those who call upon the name of our Lord Jesus Christ in every place, "their Lord and ours" (1:2c), further describes the church at Corinth as a worshiping assembly united with all other worshiping assemblies of believers in the Lord Jesus Christ.[4]

In his introductory epistolary greeting, "grace to you and peace from God our Father and the Lord Jesus Christ" (1:3), Paul reminds the Corinthians of the divine grace and peace they have already received in the past when they became believers. He also asserts that their present listening to the letter will give them a renewed experience of that grace. And he initiates the ritualistic worship of the letter, as he prays that in the future they may continue to experience that divine grace and peace as a result of having listened to the letter Paul has addressed to them. Cleverly playing on the Greek word for "grace," *charis*, Paul immediately responds to this initial greeting with an act of grateful worship that reinforces the Corinthians' reception of this divine grace. Paul states that "I thank," in Greek *eucharistō*, that is, "I gratefully acknowledge the grace" of my God always concerning you because of the "grace," the *charis*, of God given to you in Christ Jesus (1:4). Indeed, the Corinthians are not lacking in any particular form of this grace—any "spiritual gift" or "charism," in Greek *charisma* (1:7). Implicitly, Paul

3. "The language Paul uses to describe the community at Corinth, 'being sanctified' and 'holy,' is biblical. . . . To be holy is to be set apart from the profane so as to be in the service of the living God. Both terms belong to the semantic domain of the cult. . . . Having entered into the linguistic register of the cult in his formula of address, Paul will devote a major portion of his letter to issues that pertain to the cultic activity of the Christians of Corinth (chs. 8–14)" (Collins, *First Corinthians*, 46).

4. "So Paul starts by giving them a gentle nudge to remind them that their own calling to be God's people belongs to a much larger picture. In the new people that God is creating for himself in the coming age that has already dawned, the Corinthians have a share with all the saints, fellow believers 'in every place' who also 'call on the name of our Lord Jesus Christ,' that is, who have put their trust in him and pray to and worship him" (Fee, *Corinthians*, 33). "Paul's description of Christians as those who call on the name of the Lord Jesus Christ . . . may also characterize what Christians do when they come together as a worshiping assembly" (Collins, *First Corinthians*, 53).

is leading the Corinthians to likewise worship God in response to the grace they have received in their various charisms.[5]

The problem of the divisions that have arisen in the community as a result of the rivalries that have developed among them (1:10–11) are based in part on who baptized them (1:13). These divisions threaten to destroy their unity and thus disqualify the Corinthians to offer proper communal worship to God. In response to this divisive concern regarding those who may claim to be baptized in the name of Paul, Paul expresses another act of epistolary worship. He declares that "I give thanks to God that I baptized none of you except Crispus and Gaius" (1:14).

Paul then presents them with a poignant rhetorical question: "Do you not know that you are the temple of God and the Spirit of God dwells among you?[6] If anyone destroys the temple of God, God will destroy that person, for the temple of God, which you yourselves are, is holy" (3:16–17). This reinforces how the Corinthians, as those who have been made holy by God in Christ Jesus, those called to be holy ones (1:2b), are those who are specially qualified to offer worship to God. As *the* very "temple" or "sanctuary" (*naos*) of God, the preeminent place not only for the dwelling but for the worship of God, the Corinthians are empowered by the Spirit of God to offer proper worship to God. As *the* temple of God, they offer worship not only when they are gathered as an assembly for their liturgical worship, but also for their ethical worship when they live as morally upright "holy ones" outside of their liturgical gatherings.[7]

---

5. "The term *charismata* denotes the source of gifts, i.e., divine *charis* (grace) becoming concrete" (Bittlinger, *Gifts and Graces*, 20). "The language is performative insofar as the very expression of his thanks in a letter is an act of thanksgiving to God. . . . For the apostle thanksgiving is an ongoing activity. Thanksgiving is more than at attitude. It is expressed in prayer, which invokes the name of God and includes intercession" (Collins, *First Corinthians*, 57). "It is clear that incorporation into Christ has alone brought these great benefits to the Corinthians, so that their status or position in Christ is the cause for genuine thanksgiving" (Winter, "Sanctification in 1 Corinthians," 193).

6. On the emphasis within the translation that "you are *the* temple," see Fee, *God's Empowering Presence*, 115n112.

7. "The people of God continue to be the Spirit-filled community when they disperse and go about their daily affairs, but their identity as 'the temple of the Lord' finds particular expression when they gather together in Jesus' name, to experience his presence and power in their midst" (Peterson, *Engaging with God*, 202). "It is difficult to overemphasize the significance of this text [3:16–17] for Paul's understanding of

Worship in 1 Corinthians 5–7

The problem that one of their members is living in an incestuous relationship with his step-mother (5:1) has serious ramifications for the Corinthian church as a worshiping assembly. First of all, they have failed to perform the formal ritual act of mourning that indicates excommunication and enacts expulsion of this individual from the community. As Paul points out to them, "Should you not rather have mourned, so that he who practiced this deed would have been removed from your midst?" (5:2). This "mourning" is not so much figurative or a psychological disposition as it is a funerary ritual publicly performed in the worshiping assembly.[8] By performing it, the assembly indicates the "death" of this individual's membership in the community and thus his necessary removal from the assembly that he has defiled by his reprehensible behavior.[9] His removal is necessary so that the Corinthians may maintain the purity by which they may offer proper liturgical and ethical worship as the communal "temple of God," which is "holy" (3:16–17).[10]

---

the church—as primarily a people of the Spirit. This is true not only when they are thought of as a corporate reality, a kind of new race in the local setting where they are placed, but also when they are thought of as a gathered community, worshipping the living God and thereby ministering to one another. . . . The language 'holy' maintains the imagery of temple, a place set apart for God and not to be desecrated in any way. As imagery, such language no longer refers to ritual holiness, but to 'holy' in the moral-ethical sense. . . . God is holy . . . and as his temple, his people are by implication also to be holy" (Fee, *God's Empowering Presence*, 115–16). See also Lanci, *New Temple for Corinth.*

8. "Paul links mourning with removal, which has puzzled modern interpreters and pushed them to understand mourning figuratively. Yet there is no compelling reason to take the Greek verb for mourning (*pentheō*) as a reference to an inner or psychological disposition—a sense of sadness or regret—rather than ritual practice, that is, the public rite of mourning. While the verb could have an experiential side, it normally meant the mourning connected with a funeral. It clearly has this meaning in the gospels (Matt 5:4; 9:15; Mark 16:10; Luke 6:25) and in Revelation (18:11, 15, 19). Paul's reference to mourning in 1 Corinthians 5:2 should be read, therefore, as a reference to the formal actions connected with a state of mourning" (DeMaris, *Ritual World*, 82).

9. "Funerals marked exit from community, so they are functionally like expulsions. Accordingly, funeral ritual could signal execration or excommunication. More to the point, mourning could enact expulsion, which is what 1 Corinthians 5:2 indicates" (ibid., 83). "Had they mourned they would have extirpated the incestuous man from their midst" (Collins, *First Corinthians*, 210).

10. According to DeMaris (*Ritual World*, 89), the language in 1 Cor 3:16–17 "about

In the second place, in contrast to the Corinthian church, which has failed to perform the ritual of mourning that would expel the incestuous man, Paul, for his part (the Greek is emphatic: "I for my part" [*egō men gar*]), has already pronounced judgment in the name of our Lord Jesus on the one who perpetrated this deed (5:3–4a). That Paul has pronounced judgment on the individual "in the name of our Lord Jesus" makes it a ritualistic liturgical act.[11] It takes effect as a "performative speech act," that is, a pronouncement that does what it says, when the Corinthians listen to the letter that makes Paul present to them as a liturgical assembly who "call upon the name of our Lord Jesus Christ" (1:2; cf. 1:10). In other words, as they are gathered for worship, which probably includes the Eucharist, Paul, made present by the letter itself even though he is physically absent, actually enacts his judgment of this individual and makes it a reality.[12]

Furthermore, when they and an emphatic "my" (*emou*) "Spirit," that is, the Holy Spirit that dwells within Paul and the Corinthians as the holy temple of God (3:16–17), together with the power of our Lord Jesus, are gathered together as a worshiping assembly, they are to carry out and complete Paul's ritualistic pronouncement of judgment with their own performance of a ritualistic act (5:4b). They are to hand over this man to Satan, that is, publicly and officially expel him from the holy community and send him out into the profane world, the domain of the demonic power of Satan, as a ceremonial ritual of purification. This excommunication is for the destruction of "the flesh" to rid the assembly of contamination, so that "the Spirit," that is, the Corinthian assembly

---

the temple as a holy place, as God's dwelling place, and about the fate of anyone who threatens to defile the temple fully anticipates the discussion of chapter 5, where Paul stresses purity and the eliminatory rite that will achieve it." See also Rosen, "Temple and Holiness," 137–45.

11. "Paul's words would evoke the idea of a Christian assembly that invokes the name of the Lord (cf. 1:2)" (Collins, *First Corinthians*, 211).

12. "When Paul talks elsewhere in this letter about the Corinthians assembling . . . the setting is worship, presumably in a household, not administrative council or court-room (1 Cor 11:17, 18, 20, 33, 34; 14:23, 26). The numerous references in chapter 11 refer to coming together for the eucharistic meal, participation in which, Paul insists, calls for judgment (11:29, 31–2). Hence, a eucharistic setting for the ceremonial punishment seems very likely" (DeMaris, *Ritual World*, 81). See also Johnson, *Religious Experience*, 175.

in whom the Holy Spirit dwells as the holy temple of God, may be saved on the day of the Lord (5:5).[13]

And finally, the issue of the incestuous man is compared to the liturgical celebration of the Jewish feast of Passover and Unleavened Bread. Paul poignantly asks whether they know that a "little leaven," that is, the incestuous man, leavens "the whole batch of dough," that is, the Corinthian community (5:6). They are to clean out this "old leaven," so that they may be a "new batch of dough," inasmuch as they already are actually "unleavened," for indeed our "Passover lamb," Christ, has been sacrificed (5:7).[14] That they are already "unleavened" by virtue of the sacrificial death of Christ recalls that they are actually "holy ones," who have been made holy in Christ Jesus (1:2), and thus have the requisite holiness and purity to celebrate the feast. Consequently, Paul leads them in the celebration of this new, Christian feast of Passover and Unleavened Bread, as he exhorts them, "Therefore let us celebrate the feast," not with the "old leaven," the incestuous man, who is a "leaven" that ferments "wickedness and evil." Rather, we are to celebrate with the "unleavened bread," which is "purity and truth" (5:8). They may

13. "When Paul called for purification, we should assume that he had the Corinthian church in mind. Resistance to this understanding has resulted in translations and interpretations of verse 5 that make the immoral man the focal point of the rite. . . . Yet this reading does not square with Paul's anthropology: flesh and spirit were not distinct parts of the human being; they were orientations that human beings could embrace, or realms or theaters in which they could operate. More important, the Greek at the end of verse 5 does not actually say his (the man's) flesh and *his* spirit but *the* flesh and *the* spirit. . . . If the group's survival is foremost in Paul's thinking, then we need to consider verse 5 not as a statement about the fate of the offender but about the consequences of the expulsion for the group: their action will purge the community of defilement—the works of flesh embodied in the deviate—and thus preserve the community—God's spirit will continue to dwell there" (DeMaris, *Ritual World*, 86–87). "He directs the community to excise the fleshy individual—so characterized by reason of his incestuous behavior—from its midst so that the community might live under the power of the Spirit and be preserved for the day of the Lord" (Collins, *First Corinthians*, 213). This, of course, does not rule out the eventual conversion and salvation of the incestuous man, but that is not the chief concern here.

14. "The operative image of the church in this portion of the letter is that of God's holy temple (3.16–17), which suggests that what was ultimately at issue was the purity of the community. The man who was living with his father's wife must be expelled in order to maintain this purity. This concern is further expressed by the imagery of the leaven which has to be cleansed out (5.6–7)" (Pickett, *Cross in Corinth*, 109–10).

celebrate this new Passover liturgically in the Eucharist and ethically in their moral lives as Christians.[15]

With regard to the immoral practice of those Corinthians who frequent prostitutes (6:13–18), Paul asks the Corinthians whether they know that their communal body, composed of their individual bodies, is a "temple" or "sanctuary" (*naos*) of the Holy Spirit within them, which they have from God, so that they are not their own but belong to God (6:19; cf. 3:16–17). As God's own holy temple, they are to offer both liturgical and ethical worship to God. They are to conduct this worship in the form of "glorifying" God in their body—both their communal and individual bodies (6:20). And this they may do by avoiding sexual immorality, since the sexually immoral individual sins against both his individual and corporate body (6:18), rendering both of these bodies incapable of the worship that glorifies God.[16]

In addressing the issue of those Corinthians who are married to unbelievers, Paul instructs them not to divorce if the unbelieving spouse is willing to continue the marriage (7:12–13). The rationale he puts forth for this is noteworthy for the theme of worship. Paul asserts that the unbelieving spouse has been made holy in the believing spouse, who was made holy (6:11) and became one of the holy ones (1:2), when

15. "While it is a novel Passover that has Christ as the paschal lamb, the demand for purification associated with traditional Passover remains in force. Just as Israelite households have to purify themselves by getting rid of all leaven, so too must the Corinthian assembly. Since one could not celebrate Passover with the old yeast—Paul adds—'of malice and evil,' the embodiment of those vices among the Corinthians, the immoral man, has to go. In these verses Paul invokes the requirements of cultic preparation to convince the Corinthian community to cleanse itself" (DeMaris, *Ritual World*, 84–85). "The Church now, by virtue of celebrating its own Passover, exists in a covenantal relationship with God. Christ, its own paschal lamb, has been sacrificed and it lives as if during the festival. Its members, in Paul's words, are the new dough, the unleavened bread untainted by the old, the presence of which would prevent the proper celebration of the festival" (Newton, *Concept of Purity*, 93).

16. "With a nice *double entendre* Paul exhorts the Corinthians to cleave to the Lord (and thus *his* body, the church) instead of cleaving (sexually) with prostitutes. Because the Christian belongs not to her or himself (6:19), but rather to the Lord and thus to his body, the church, the claim that 'one can do anything' cannot be the sole standard of conduct. In this short passage Paul draws on still another image of the church, the building image, which was prepared for already in chap. 3. Here its application is simultaneously individualistic and corporate ('your body is the temple of the holy spirit in you'). Not individual advantage but God's glory should be the measuring rod for Christian decision-making" (Mitchell, *Paul and the Rhetoric of Reconciliation*, 234).

he or she became a believer. Furthermore, even their children are holy (7:14).[17] That the entire family has been made "holy" by virtue of the believing spouse, then, assimilates it within the believing community as the "holy" temple of God (3:16–17). Not only does the unbelieving spouse not defile or disqualify the worship of the believing spouse, but because the whole family is, in fact, "holy," the implication is that all of its members, spouses as well as children, may participate in both the liturgical and ethical worship appropriate to the Corinthian church as God's holy temple.[18]

Worship in 1 Corinthians 8–11

Another issue involving worship is the question of eating meat that has been sacrificed to idols in the pagan temples at Corinth. Paul warns that those Corinthians who have the knowledge that idols are nothing, since there is no God but the one God (8:1–6), not lead those who do not have this knowledge into idolatry.[19] When those who do not have this knowledge and who have been accustomed to idolatry in the past eat meat sacrificed to idols, their weak conscience is defiled (8:7) and they are thus led back into idolatry. For if someone sees one who has this knowledge reclining at table in the temple of an idol, his weak conscience may be provoked to lead him to likewise recline at table to eat the meat that has been sacrificed to idols (8:10). Such an individual would again become engaged in the false worship of idolatry.

But Paul is concerned that even those with the knowledge that idols are nothing may also fall into idolatry by eating the meat sacrificed to

17. Martens, "First Corinthians 7:14," 31–35.

18. "The Christian united to Christ brings the non-Christian partner into a power sphere of holiness that somehow neutralizes the non-Chrisitan's potential to contaminate the Christian. . . . Contending that the Christian wife has the same power to sanctify her unbelieving husband as the Christian husband has to sanctify his unbelieving wife is quite novel. It accords with Paul's emphasis throughout the chapter on the mutuality of spouses, but it also expresses his conviction that Christians live in a new and potent field of God's holiness that works irrespective of gender" (Garland, *1 Corinthians*, 288–89). "Paul's idea of the 'holiness' of mixed marriage retains the cultic overtones of holiness language that has been present in his letter since 1:2. Holiness means belonging to God. It describes what is according to God's plan and design" (Collins, *First Corinthians*, 267).

19. Nicholson, *Dynamic Oneness*, 35–104.

idols. He informs his Corinthian audience that "our fathers," that is, our Israelite ancestors in the Exodus event, were all "baptized" into Moses in the cloud and in the sea (10:1–2), thus anticipating the sacramental ritual by which the Corinthians were "baptized" into Christ (1:13). Furthermore, our Israelite ancestors all ate the same spiritual food, and they all drank the same spiritual drink, for they were drinking from a spiritual rock following them, a rock that was the Christ (10:3–4). This anticipates the sacramental ritual of the Lord's Supper practiced by the Corinthians.[20] But as God was "displeased," and thus not properly worshiped, by most of the Israelites, so that they were struck down in the desert (10:5), so the ominous implication for the Corinthians is that God may likewise be displeased and not properly worshiped by them despite their having performed the sacramental rituals of baptism and the Eucharist.

Consequently, the Corinthians are not to become idolaters like many of their Israelite ancestors, as it is written, "the people sat down to eat and drink and stood up to play" (10:7; cf. Exod 32:6b). All of the Israelite ancestors, that is, all of the people of God, partook of the same spiritual food and drink, drinking from the spiritual rock that was the Christ (10:3–4). Nevertheless, some of them, as "the people" of God, sat down to eat and drink from the peace offerings that had been sacrificed to the idolatrous golden calf and then, as disparate and rebellious individuals, "stood up" to the further idolatrous behavior of "playing" before the golden calf. The craving for and partaking of idolatrous sacrificial food and drink on the part of some of them contradicted the unity of all who shared the same spiritual food and drink in the desert. Paul thus warns that those Corinthians who eat the meat sacrificed to idols not only may lead others into idolatry but also will become idolaters themselves and thus contradict their status as the holy temple of God (3:16–17), set apart for the worship of the one God and the one Lord (8:6).[21]

Paul thus urges the Corinthians to "flee" from the idolatry of eating meat sacrificed to idols (10:14), since it is completely incompatible with

20. "Paul describes Israel's experience of the miraculous bread (Exod. 16:4–30) and miraculous drinking of water from the rock (Exod. 17:1–17; Num. 20:2–13) as a form of 'spiritual eating,' unquestionably viewing it as a type/analogy of the Lord's Supper" (Fee, *Corinthians*, 446).

21. Heil, *1 Corinthians*, 145–59.

their eating of the eucharistic meal. At the Eucharist the cup of blessing that is blessed is a communion in the blood of Christ and the bread that is broken is a communion in the body of Christ, for those who partake of this one bread become one body (10:16–17). The Eucharist thus unites its participants to one another and to Christ in a "fellowship" or "communion" (*koinōnia*; cf. 1:9). But, since the meat sacrificed in pagan temples is offered to demonic idols, Paul does not want the Corinthians to be in a communion with demons. The Corinthians cannot drink the cup of the Lord and the cup of demons; they cannot partake of the table of the Lord and the table of demons (10:20–21). Whether they eat or drink, or whatever they do, they are to do everything for the "glory of God" (10:31), that is, for the glory that offers proper liturgical as well as ethical worship to God. By their eating and drinking at the Eucharist celebrated within their worshiping assembly, without also eating the food sacrificed to demonic idols outside of their assembly, they will give glory to and properly worship God both liturgically and ethically.[22]

Another concern of Paul is that the church at Corinth conforms with all of the other churches (4:17; 7:17) and that they avoid giving offense to the church of God (10:32). In order for the Corinthians truly to be a church of God that does everything for the "glory of God" (10:31), that is, for the proper worship of God, they too must behave, while praying or prophesying in communal worship, in accord with the scriptural order of God's creation (11:3–15). This is the custom for the communal worship that takes place in all of the other churches (11:16). Men and women are to wear the hairstyles proper to their gender out of respect for themselves as individuals (11:4, 5–6, 13, 14, 15), for one another as men and women (11:8–9, 11–12), for the other churches (11:16), and for the angels (11:10), Christ (11:3), and God (11:3, 7, 12). They must include the practice of this custom in their liturgical gatherings in order to worship God properly by doing everything for the glory of God.[23]

---

22. According to Fee (*Corinthians*, 488n62), "for the glory of God" here "means to his praise, i.e., so that the believer's actions will bring him glory, honor, and praise." See also Newman, *Paul's Glory Christology*, 157–63.

23. Heil, *1 Corinthians*, 173–90. "It seems self-evident that the custom to which Paul alludes concerns gender distinction in public worship . . . addressed both to men and women equally. The custom is the acceptance of an equality of status in accordance with which woman may lead in public prayer or preaching side by side with a recognition that gender differences must not be blurred but appreciated, valued, and

Next Paul addresses an abuse that takes place when the Corinthians come together as a worshiping assembly to eat the Lord's Supper. Before the communal eating of this eucharistic meal some of those who have gathered are eating and drinking at their own individual suppers. This results in a situation of some going hungry while others are getting drunk (11:21)! They should be eating these suppers in their own houses, rather than showing contempt for the church of God and shaming those who do not have their own suppers (11:22). Such behavior is not appropriate for the Lord's Supper, as Paul reminds them "that the Lord Jesus on the night in which he was betrayed took the bread, and, giving thanks, broke it and said, 'This is my body that is for you. Do this in remembrance of me.' Likewise also the cup after supper, saying, 'This cup is the new covenant in my blood. Do this, as often as you drink it, in remembrance of me.' For as often as you eat this bread and drink the cup, you proclaim the death of the Lord until he comes" (11:23–26). Therefore, as Paul warns, whoever eats the bread and drinks the cup of the Lord unworthily will be guilty of the body and blood of the Lord (11:27) when the Lord comes again for the final judgment.

Consequently, before participating in the communal worship that takes place in the Lord's Supper, each individual should undergo self-examination before eating of the bread and drinking of the cup (11:28). For whoever eats and drinks without discerning the "body" eats and drinks judgment on oneself (11:29), in accord with the future orientation of the Lord's Supper at which the community proclaims the death of the Lord until he comes again to conduct the final judgment (11:26). Not discerning the "body" means not recognizing that those who partake of the bread are in a communion with one another and with the "body" of Christ. Although they may be many, they become one "body" (10:16–17). Those individuals who go ahead with their own suppers before the Lord's Supper thus contradict the communal unity of the participants that is its purpose. Therefore, Paul urges the Corinthians that when they come together to eat, they are to wait for and welcome one another into this communal coming together for worship (11:33).[24]

---

expressed in appropriate ways in response to God's unrevoked decree" (Thiselton, *Corinthians*, 847).

24. "The Corinthians are missing the meaning of the 'body' given in death, but Paul's present concern is with the further sense, the church as that body" (Fee, *Corinthians*, 564). "The [Lord's] body has as its referent the eucharistic body, but Paul